# Engineering Marvels

# The Eiffel TOWER

Measurement

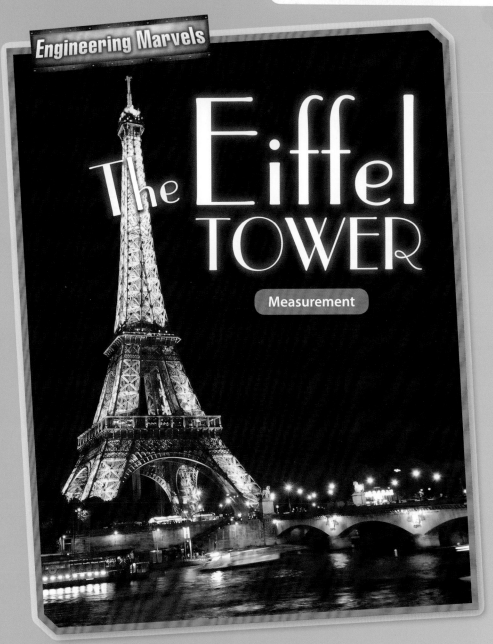

Dona Herweck Rice

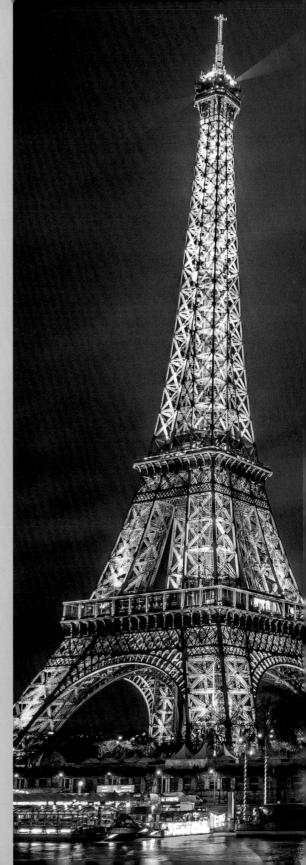

## Consultants

**Michele Ogden, Ed.D**
Principal
Irvine Unified School District

**Colleen Pollitt, M.A.Ed.**
Math Support Teacher
Howard County Public Schools

**Publishing Credits**

Rachelle Cracchiolo, M.S.Ed., *Publisher*
Conni Medina, M.A.Ed., *Managing Editor*
Dona Herweck Rice, *Series Developer*
Emily R. Smith, M.A.Ed., *Series Developer*
Diana Kenney, M.A.Ed., NBCT, *Content Director*
Stacy Monsman, M.A., *Editor*
Kevin Panter, *Graphic Designer*

**Image Credits:** p.5 (inset) World History Archive/Alamy Stock Photo, (full page) DeAgostini/M. Seemuller/Getty Images; pp.6–7 Markus Schieder/Alamy Stock Photo; p.7 (bottom) Photo12/UIG/Getty Images; pp.8, 9 Chronicle/Alamy Stock Photo; p.10 Prisma Archivo/Alamy Stock Photo; pp.10–11 Sueddeutsche Zeitung Photo/Alamy Stock Photo; p.12 Chronicle/Alamy Stock Photo; p.12–13 Etabeta/Alamy Stock Photo; pp.14–15 FL Collection 2/Alamy Stock Photo; p.16 FPG/Hulton Archive/Getty Images; p.17 Philippe Bataillon/INA via Getty Images; pp.18–19 Keystone-France/Getty Images; p.20 FPG/Getty Images; p.22 ullstein bild via Getty Images; p.25 SSPL/Getty Images; all other images from iStock and/or Shutterstock.

**Library of Congress Cataloging-in-Publication Data**

Names: Rice, Dona, author.
Title: Engineering marvels : the Eiffel Tower / Dona Herweck Rice.
Description: Huntington Beach, CA : Teacher Created Materials, 2017. | Includes index. | Audience: Grades 4 to 6.
Identifiers: LCCN 2017012138 (print) | LCCN 2017012799 (ebook) | ISBN 9781480759411 (eBook) | ISBN 9781425855598 (pbk.)
Subjects: LCSH: Tour Eiffel (Paris, France)--Juvenile literature. | Eiffel, Gustave, 1832-1923--Juvenile literature. | Paris (France)--Buildings, structures, etc.--Juvenile literature.
Classification: LCC NA2930 (ebook) | LCC NA2930 .R53 2017 (print) | DDC 720.944/361--dc23
LC record available at https://lccn.loc.gov/2017012138

## Teacher Created Materials

5301 Oceanus Drive
Huntington Beach, CA 92649-1030
http://www.tcmpub.com

### ISBN 978-1- 4258-5559-8
© 2018 Teacher Created Materials, Inc.
Printed in China WAI002

# Table of Contents

# World's Fair, 1889

The world was changing, and there was no better place to see the change than at the World's Fair. From May 5 to October 21, the World's Fair was the talk of Paris, France. It was the place everyone wanted to be. Countries around the world exhibited there. Visitors to the fair felt as though they had visited the world! They also had a chance to experience what was new and bizarre. A building with **mechanized** parts? The World's Fair had it. A pavilion just for demonstrating good hygiene? You could find it at the fair. Fifty tons of cheese to be enjoyed by visitors each week? Yes, the fair had that, too.

Something different and exciting was everywhere a person looked. Even so, what visitors most wanted to see was the new building by Gustave Eiffel and his team. They thought it was **outrageous**. The French call it the *Tour Eiffel*. We know it as the Eiffel Tower. Today, it stands for France itself. No visit to Paris is complete without a trip to the pointed tower that stands tall over the historic city.

Gustave Eiffel

# LET'S EXPLORE MATH

In 1889, the Eiffel Tower was the tallest building in the world. It stands about 300 meters tall. Would the tower's height in centimeters be greater than or less than 300? Explain your reasoning.

People visit the 1889 World's Fair in Paris, France.

This is the view of the Champ-de-Mars as seen from the Eiffel Tower.

# Eiffel Builds a Tower

The Storming of the Bastille in 1789 marked the start of the French Revolution. The World's Fair was set in Paris in 1889 to mark the 100-year anniversary of that important battle. The people of France no longer wanted to be ruled by a monarch. They began a new age of **democracy**.

To honor the event, **engineers** were asked to submit plans to erect a tower. It would be built at the Champ-de-Mars (shaw-duh-mahrs). The Champ-de-Mars is a long park in Paris. It is named after Mars, the Roman god of war. The park was first used as a site for military drills.

The tower was meant to have a square base. It would be 300 meters (984 feet) tall and 125 meters (410 feet) wide. It would also serve as a model of modern engineering. More than 100 plans were submitted. A man named Gustave Eiffel and his team developed one of those plans. Their plan was chosen. They had just over two years to build the tower. But could they do it? Nothing like it had ever been built before.

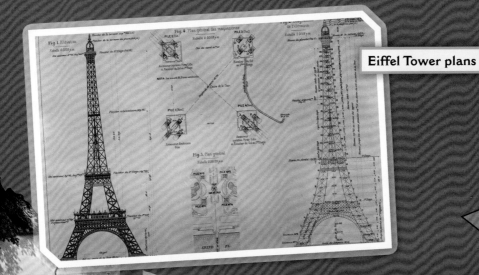

Eiffel Tower plans

# Breaking Ground and Laying a Foundation

Eiffel's project began in January of 1887. His workers dug the square foundation that would **anchor** the tower. They carved a large hole about 15 m (49 ft.) into the ground. They used only shovels to dig the hole!

The workers filled about 6 m (19 ft.) of that space with concrete and stone. Eiffel used fast-drying cement to deal with the wet soil. He also used different methods to build each side of the foundation. One side of the soil was wetter than the other. Eiffel dug the wetter side deeper. He also used materials that were often used to build bridges. (Part of every bridge is underwater.)

Soil conditions make a big difference in the materials used. They also make a difference in whether a structure can stand at all. Very soft or wet soil may not hold the structure's weight. It may tip or break if the soil is not right.

It took a lot of work to get the tower's foundation as it should be. In all, about four months went into the process.

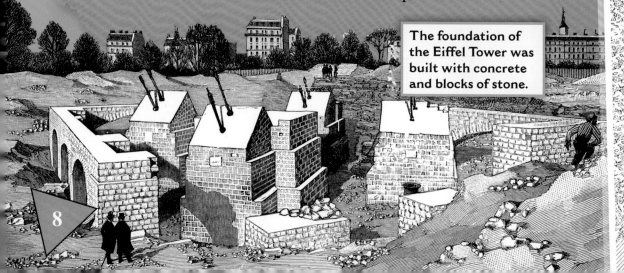

The foundation of the Eiffel Tower was built with concrete and blocks of stone.

cutaway view showing the underground foundation work, tubing access, and clearing with compressed air

# Piece by Piece

Every piece of the tower was built in Eiffel's factory. Each piece was **meticulously** crafted. If the measurement of any piece was off by even a little, the tower would be a failure. The pieces were checked and rechecked. Eiffel had to be sure.

There are 18,000 pieces that make up the tower. About 100 workers were needed just to craft the pieces. About twice that number put the pieces together. Some people say the tower is like a giant Erector Set™! The pieces fit like a puzzle with everything in its proper place. The workers used a series of scaffolds to help build the tower with precision from the ground up.

The tower stands on four legs. The legs are angled. Eiffel said that the angle of the legs allows wind to pass through the tower without causing damage. Each leg faces north, south, east, or west. The legs are bolted to the foundation. Huge bolts were used to secure the tower. Each one is about 8 m (26 ft.) long and 10 cm (4 in.) around!

Men work to construct the Eiffel Tower.

Eiffel Tower under construction in 1888

## LET'S EXPLORE MATH

Each bolt used to secure the tower was 26 feet long. How many inches long was each bolt? Complete the table to show your answer.

| Feet | Inches |
|------|--------|
| 1    | 12     |
| 26   |        |

Workers heat and hammer rivets to replace the bolts of the Eiffel Tower in 1889.

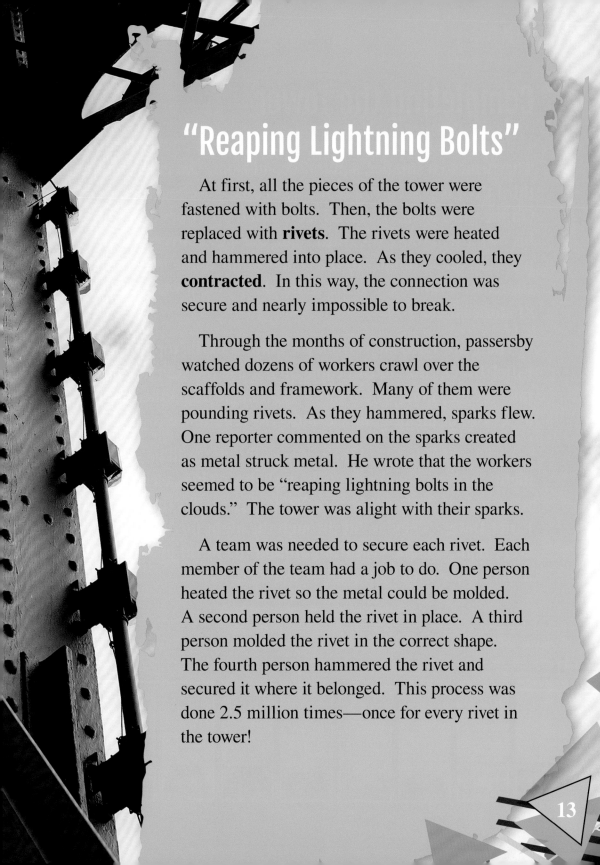

# "Reaping Lightning Bolts"

At first, all the pieces of the tower were fastened with bolts. Then, the bolts were replaced with **rivets**. The rivets were heated and hammered into place. As they cooled, they **contracted**. In this way, the connection was secure and nearly impossible to break.

Through the months of construction, passersby watched dozens of workers crawl over the scaffolds and framework. Many of them were pounding rivets. As they hammered, sparks flew. One reporter commented on the sparks created as metal struck metal. He wrote that the workers seemed to be "reaping lightning bolts in the clouds." The tower was alight with their sparks.

A team was needed to secure each rivet. Each member of the team had a job to do. One person heated the rivet so the metal could be molded. A second person held the rivet in place. A third person molded the rivet in the correct shape. The fourth person hammered the rivet and secured it where it belonged. This process was done 2.5 million times—once for every rivet in the tower!

# Completing the Tower

From the square first floor, the tower's legs angle upward. They lead to a smaller, square second floor. An even smaller third floor is placed where the legs come close together. On the third floor, Eiffel added a small apartment for his own use. Above the third floor, the legs **converge** to a platform and a dome. In the center of the dome is a spiral staircase. From the ground to the dome, the tower is about 81 stories high.

There are 1,665 steps from the bottom to the top of the Eiffel Tower. But, most people do not use the stairs. They take the elevators, which move at an angle along the tower's legs. Two of the original elevators are still in use.

Eiffel added lights to the tower so that it could be seen at night. At first, there were only gaslights. Then, electric lights were added. Today, there are 20,000 light bulbs that cover the Eiffel Tower. They are lit through the night for 10 minutes every hour. People visit from around the world just to see the tower ablaze with light against the night sky.

photographic time line of
Eiffel Tower construction

August, 1887

14

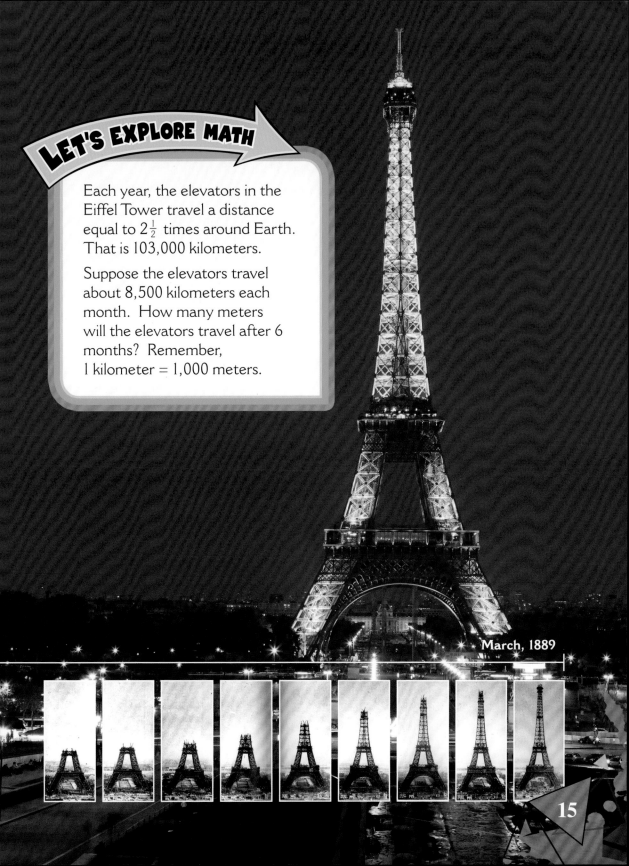

Each year, the elevators in the Eiffel Tower travel a distance equal to $2\frac{1}{2}$ times around Earth. That is 103,000 kilometers.

Suppose the elevators travel about 8,500 kilometers each month. How many meters will the elevators travel after 6 months? Remember, 1 kilometer = 1,000 meters.

March, 1889

# The Final Touches

To protect the metal, the tower was painted. Twelve thousand gallons of paint were used. That is about 60 tons of paint! In fact, that much paint is needed every seven years. That is how often the tower must be repainted. The job takes up to 18 months to complete each time!

**A man paints a section of the Eiffel Tower in 1939.**

## LET'S EXPLORE MATH

Suppose one worker paints a section of the tower. He uses 15 gallons of paint. Another worker uses 4 times the amount of paint. How many quarts of paint does the second worker use? Show your thinking. Note: 1 gallon = 4 quarts.

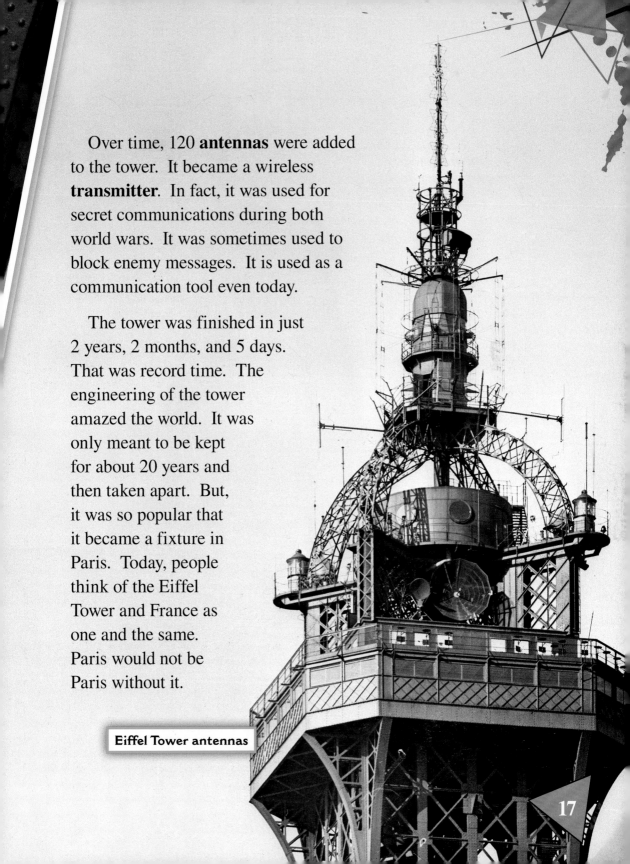

Over time, 120 **antennas** were added to the tower. It became a wireless **transmitter**. In fact, it was used for secret communications during both world wars. It was sometimes used to block enemy messages. It is used as a communication tool even today.

The tower was finished in just 2 years, 2 months, and 5 days. That was record time. The engineering of the tower amazed the world. It was only meant to be kept for about 20 years and then taken apart. But, it was so popular that it became a fixture in Paris. Today, people think of the Eiffel Tower and France as one and the same. Paris would not be Paris without it.

Eiffel Tower antennas

Crowds walk beneath
the Eiffel Tower in 1900.

# The World Comes to Eiffel

At first, the people of France did not love the tower. They were **drawn** to it, but many thought it was an eyesore. In fact, a petition was started to stop it from being built. Some people thought it was more of a joke than a work of art. They called it "useless and monstrous." Nothing like it had ever been seen before. Paris is an old city filled with grand architecture. The modern design of the tower did not fit with many people's idea of French beauty.

But, construction continued. And, it did not take long for most minds to change. Today, the Eiffel Tower is thought of as a masterpiece. It is the most visited man-made structure in the world that people pay to see. About 7 million people go there each year! More than 250 million people have visited it since it first opened. The most common guests are from France and nearby countries. They make up nearly half of all visitors. About 8 out of every 100 visitors are from the United States. It is a rare tourist who goes to Paris without seeing the tower.

# Fascinating Facts

Because the Eiffel Tower is famous, people use it for stunts. The first stair-climbing contest was held in 1905. People ran as fast as they could to the second floor. The winner did it in 3 minutes and 12 seconds. In 1923, someone rode a bike down the stairs. In 1935, a stuntman balanced himself on a handrail at the very top of the tower. In 1987, a bungee jumper leaped from it. Two years later, Philippe Petit walked a wire between the tower and another building. In 2005, a man in a wheelchair rolled down the stairs from the first floor. All these people achieved what they tried to do. A few pilots of small airplanes have even flown under the tower arches. Not all of them lived to tell the story!

Many people do not have a way to visit the tower. It is too far for them to travel. So, some places have built **replicas** of it. The one in Las Vegas is a popular tourist spot. Several others are in Asia. One in China and another in Japan are even built to **scale**.

Eiffel Tower replica in Las Vegas

Gustave Eiffel poses with a model of the Eiffel Tower in the early 1900s.

# The Man Himself

Eiffel's plan for the tower was to build a structure as strong as stone but with less weight. While the structure is heavy, it would be heavier if built from normal materials. Also, the metal framework is wind resistant. Eiffel figured that the angle at which the legs are built offers maximum resistance. It is part of what allows the tower to stand as securely as it does.

Gustave Eiffel is famous for more than just the tower he made. He also created the metal frame of another icon. It was given to the United States as a gift from France. This icon is the Statue of Liberty.

But, not everything Eiffel did was a success. His reputation suffered when he designed locks for the Panama Canal. A builder botched the job, but Eiffel was caught in the bad press. He was sentenced to prison for fraud! But, he fought the charges and cleared his name. Even so, his reputation was hurt. The **flak** he received over the tower wore him down as well. He gave up his work.

Statue of Liberty

a lock in the Panama Canal

23

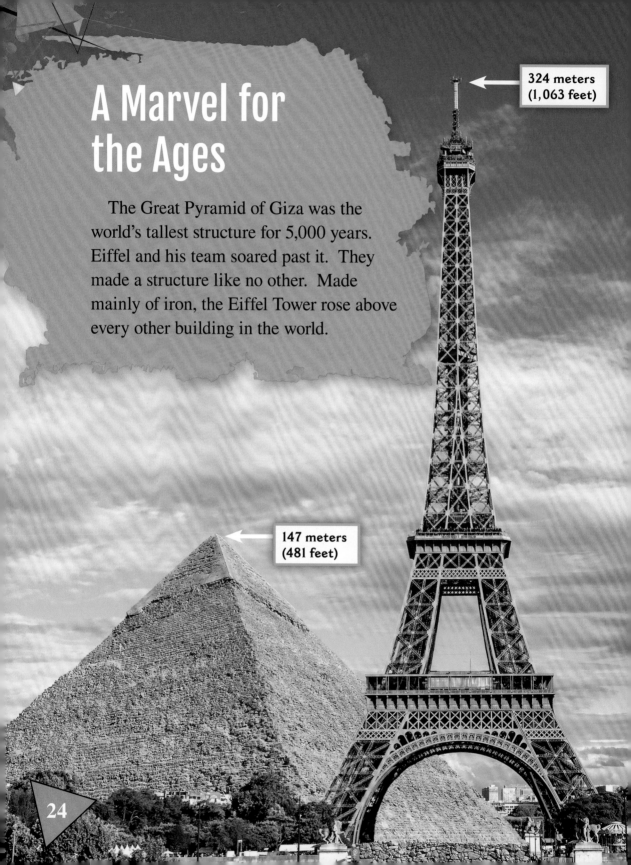

# A Marvel for the Ages

The Great Pyramid of Giza was the world's tallest structure for 5,000 years. Eiffel and his team soared past it. They made a structure like no other. Made mainly of iron, the Eiffel Tower rose above every other building in the world.

324 meters (1,063 feet)

147 meters (481 feet)

Each piece that went into the tower was made by hand.  It was also lightweight.  It was much lighter than any regular structure might have been.  That helped with the issue of gravity for such a tall building.  The way that it was shaped also gave it huge appeal.  The shape made it highly wind resistant, too.  Eiffel and his team created more than 5,000 drawings to guide them as they built.  Their planning was perfect.  So were their measurements.  No part of the tower had to be redone.

When the tower became used as a radio transmitter, people saw its full value.  A new antenna raised its height to 324 m (1,063 ft.).  The Eiffel Tower remains the tallest structure in Paris.  It is among the 30 tallest buildings in the world.  It is by far the oldest structure on that list.

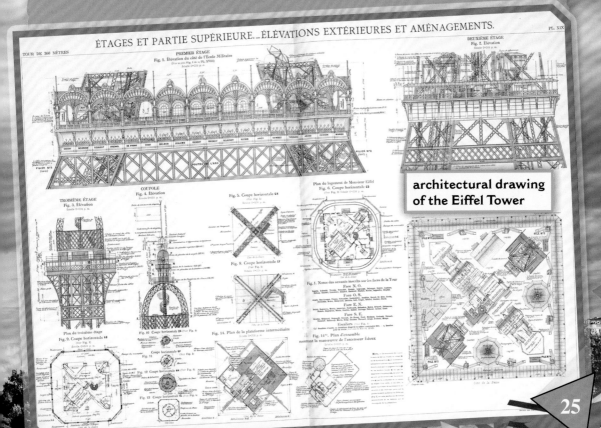

architectural drawing of the Eiffel Tower

Climbing the new tower, millions of visitors saw something they had never seen before. They saw Earth from a point high above it. Modern people have many chances to look at the world from high above. But not so in the late 1800s. People were awed.

They were awed, too, by how easily the Eiffel Tower can adapt. It can change in extreme weather. In high heat and sunlight, the tower leans about 18 cm (7 in.) away from the sun. In cold weather, the metal shrinks about 15 cm (6 in.). When winds are strong, the top of the tower can sway about 18 cm (7 in.). Imagine being on the upper part of the tower when it sways! But the tower never breaks or falls. It is not weakened.

Eiffel's tower is a marvel of engineering. Modern engineers think of it as one of their field's great achievements. People of Eiffel's time thought so, too. He was awarded the French Legion of Honor—and a tower that would forever bear his name.

gold bust of Gustave Eiffel

Imagine that on a hot summer day, the Eiffel Tower leans 12 centimeters away from the sun. The next day, it leans 90 millimeters away from the sun. How many more millimeters does the tower lean on the first day? Note: 1 centimeter = 10 millimeters.

# ⚙️ Problem Solving

Gustave Eiffel and his team had to be exact with their measurements. One mistake, and the tower could collapse. Each piece depended on the other pieces. Eiffel worked carefully to be sure all measurements measured up!

Imagine you are an engineer building a replica of the Eiffel Tower. You want to organize the pieces by placing them in ascending order. That means the pieces must be ordered from shortest length to longest length.

Use the given measurements for each piece to complete the table. Then, order the pieces from shortest to longest. Remember, 1 yard = 3 feet and 1 foot = 12 inches.

| Yards | Feet | Inches |
|:-----:|:----:|:------:|
| 2 | | |
| | | 36 |
| | 4 | |
| 5 | | |
| | 7 | |

# Glossary

**anchor**—hold steady; provide support

**antennas**—devices for sending out and receiving radio or television signals

**contracted**—became or made smaller

**converge**—come together as one

**democracy**—a form of government in which the people make laws and choose leaders through a process of voting

**drawn**—pulled or attracted to

**engineers**—people trained to build machines, structures, and systems

**flak**—criticism

**mechanized**—done by machine

**meticulously**—with fine attention to detail

**outrageous**—beyond the limits of what is reasonable

**replicas**—copies

**rivets**—special pins or bolts used to join two pieces of metal

**scale**—the relationship between measurements on models and actual measurements

**transmitter**—a device for sending out radio or television signals

# Index

# Answer Key

## Let's Explore Math

**page 5:**

Greater than 300; Explanations will vary, but should include that a centimeter is a smaller unit of measure than a meter, so there will be more centimeters than meters when expressing the height of the tower.

**page 11:**

312 inches
26 × 12 = 312

**page 15:**

51,000,000 meters
8,500 × 6 = 51,000
51,000 × 1,000 = 51,000,000

**page 16:**

240 quarts
15 × 4 = 60
60 × 4 = 240

**page 27:**

30 millimeters
12 centimeters = 120 millimeters
120 − 90 = 30

## Problem Solving

Ascending order: 36 inches, 4 feet, 2 yards, 7 feet, and 5 yards

| Yards | Feet | Inches |
|-------|------|--------|
| 2 | 6 | 72 |
| 1 | 3 | 36 |
| $1\frac{1}{3}$ | 4 | 48 |
| 5 | 15 | 180 |
| $2\frac{1}{3}$ | 7 | 84 |